Simple, Practical, HYPNOSIS

Simple,

Practical,

HYPNOSIS

By M. Alexander

Table of Contents

Warning

If you suffer from epilepsy or any similar medical condition, or if you can't
play video games without feeling dizzy or have a tendency to pass out, etc.
DO NOT use any of the relaxa-
tion/visualization techniques or inductions offered up in this book. Do
not try hypnosis at all if you suffer
from any of these conditions.
Also, do not try to relieve any pain
through suggestion without first consulting a medical doctor and having a
thorough examination conducted to
find out whether there might be an
underlying cause for the pain.
It is best to consult with a medical
doctor in any case before trying hyp-

nosis. Check with the doctor to find out what his or her opinion might be regarding hypnosis, especially if you are in therapy for any mental condition or ailment. For example, if you are being treated for anxiety or depression, definitely consult your doctor.

What is Hypnosis?

The terms Hypnosis and Hypnotism (derived from the Greek word for sleep, *hypnos*) were coined in the 1840s by a British physician named James Braid. Due to hypnotized subjects often closing their eyes because of a feeling of heaviness caused by eyestrain, Braid along with many others equated the trance state to sleep. In truth, however, as Braid soon realized after more study, the trance state of hypnosis is NOT sleep. The subject in trance state is acutely aware and highly suggestible, not at all like sleep in any real sense.

Braid tried to re-coin *hypnotism* to the term *monoidism*, but was unsuccessful. Hypnotism stuck.

So, hypnosis is, for all practical purposes, no more than *a state of heightened suggestibility.*

Should I be Afraid?

Well, No. . . Or perhaps, . . . Maybe.
If someone hypnotizes you and suggests that you are a stiff board, and they then suggest that you lie with your head on one chair and your feet on another and then they try to stand or sit on you, then yes, be very afraid. But hopefully no one is doing that stunt anymore. That is extremely dangerous. It was apparently a stunt that was prevalent in the 1950s. Be very afraid in that case.

The only other fear you might feel is due to how hypnosis is portrayed in old movies, where a Svengali type character is shown to completely take over the mind of another individual. This Svengali is portrayed as having complete control of this "weaker" individual and supposedly gets them to commit acts against their will—acts that the person would not commit if they weren't under the "spell" of the "mastermind" hypnotist. It's fake! All of it.

No one can completely take over your mind and get you to perform acts against your will while you are in a hypnotic state. It won't happen. If someone suggests that you do something that goes against your morals or other strong beliefs you hold, etc., you'll simply refuse and come up out of hypnosis. You'll wake up.

Now, having said that, if you are someone who would be apt to do something wild and crazy in the waking state (not hypnotized), like take off all of your clothes and run around naked, then you would have no problem doing something like that under hypnosis.

Robbing a bank or committing murder? Highly doubtful!

Someone convincing you to have sex with them? Hmm, probably not. Unless, of course, you were attracted to that person in the first place. I do suppose that the person could "suggest" that they were your boy-friend/girlfriend, or husband or wife, or get you to perceive them as such while you were under. Still, I doubt it. You would probably wake up.

In any event, there has to be a certain amount of trust or rapport between subject and hypnotist in the first place. You have to trust the hypnotist, or you won't relax and go under. I would think that you would suspect or sense that something was up pretty quickly if any funny business started. Almost everyone under hypnosis knows and is very aware of what is going on. You are not "asleep" and out of it. Your senses are heightened, your focus intensified. Per-haps your eyes are closed and your arms are feeling heavy, your body deeply relaxed, and you are lethargic. You just don't care. Unless, someone suggests you do some-thing against your will, or some other danger arises (fire would be one example), then you would wake up.

So . . .

You decide.

Whether to be afraid.

But when it comes down to it,

All Hypnosis is Self-Hypnosis!

So, there is really no reason to be afraid. You are either a willing participant, or you are not. If you are not a willing participant you will not go under.
If you've ever seen a stage hypnotist at work, you'll notice that they perform **suggestibility tests** to see who is more com-

pliant or suggestible. One of these tests might be to get volunteers to close their eyes while holding their arms straight out in front and parallel to the floor. The hypnotist will then ask these volunteers to imagine that one arm is weighted down with heavy objects, while the opposite arm has a string attached to the wrist, and the other end of this string has a bunch of helium filled balloons attached to it. The hypnotist will then suggest that the helium balloons are rising and pulling the one arm up higher and higher, while the other arm is getting heavier and heavier and being pulled downward. Then, after a couple of minutes of this, he might ask the participants to open their eyes to notice the difference in the position of one arm in relation to the other.

You better believe that he noticed which participants have the wider spread between the arms. These are the ones who are more compliant, or more interested in playing along. These are the ones more likely to follow the suggestions. The ones with the narrow arm spread are going to be asked to return to their seats.

Often times the hypnotist will perform a couple of "suggestibility tests" like this. Obviously, the more compliant subjects will make the best subjects. There might even be a natural somnambulistic subject in the group. This is someone who is so highly suggestible that they go very, very deep easily and quickly. This may or may not be a good thing, depending. The hypnotist doesn't want someone to go so deep that he or she becomes totally lethargic and unresponsive and simply falls asleep.

The depth of trance doesn't really matter. A medium to light trance works just fine in most cases. This is probably the most prevalent state. Though, too, there is a variance during the trance state. A subject is never locked at one constant level the whole time. Also, a person might be totally not compliant on one particular day and then be a highly suggestible subject on the next. Often times it depends on the individual's mood or state of mind at any given time. This all leads me to another question you might have.

What if I can't come out of a trance?

This won't happen. If a subject won't wake up on the first try, the hypnotist simply suggests again that the subject awaken. Usually, there is a count involved. The following might be an example:

"As I count upward from one to three, you will come up out of your relaxed state. On the count of three, you will awaken. One . . . Two . . . Three . . . Wake up! You are wide awake now and feeling refreshed and wonderful."

If someone doesn't come up at this point, the hypnotist merely repeats the procedure. The second time usually works. The only reason someone wouldn't come awake immediately is because he or she is too comfortable where they are and doesn't want to come up. Worst case scenario is that this person falls into sleep from here and then wakes up after a few minutes, having had a pleasant nap.

There are no worries in regard to this last question.

I hope I've covered all of the main questions. The basic ones at least. A person can always come up with reasons to be fearful about most anything.

However, having said this, I should mention that there are extremely rare cases of someone having what is called an *Abreaction*. This is where someone has some deep-seated trauma in their past and they have blocked it out to the point that they are completely unaware of it. This traumatic event comes to light in the subject's mind and he or she becomes anxious. There is the possibility of tears, panic, and/or hysteria. But like I said, this is rare. However, if this does happen the hypnotist should know how to handle this situation. The hypnotist should remain calm and advise the subject that he or she has the ability to back away from the incident and that the whole scene is receding and will "fade away," and he or she can come up out of hypnosis easily and quickly. The person should then be advised to contact a local, licensed medical doctor who is experienced in handling mental trauma.

Often times, to head off any unforeseen problems from the start, the hypnotist should advise, or suggest to each subject in hypnosis that whatever he or she is experiencing will not be harmful in any way. The subject should be advised that he or she, should anything extremely traumatic arise, will have the power to immediately disassociate from the situation and will be able to simply view it as though the situation is playing out on a movie screen and that he or she will have no sense of feeling involved in the playing out of this scene. The subject should be advised that any time they want to come up out of hypnosis all they have to do is open their eyes and they are immediately awake.

Hypnosis is really pretty simple.
The truth is we are all moving in and out of trance states all day long every day. For example, driving down the road and daydreaming, or thinking about something else is a trance state. Have you ever had someone talking to you and your mind wanders to something else, perhaps to some problem or a different conversation you had earlier. This person might ask if you heard

what he or she said. You might have caught some of it, maybe. It is all about focus. Just remember, you have to want to participate to be hypnotized, as the basic rule is that All Hypnosis is Self-Hypnosis!

Relaxation, Visualization, Repetition

Let's start with the three main parts of hypnosis listed above.

First, you'll **Relax**. A hypnotist will ask you to lie back and make yourself comfortable. This might consist of you lying on a couch, or reclining in a recliner. You'll want to take your shoes off and or loosen your clothing a little. Just make sure there is no binding clothing, etc. This loosening of clothing is probably best if you are at home and practicing self-hypnosis in privacy. But you can still get as comfortable as you can in the hypnotist's or therapist's office.

Next, you'll be asked to close your eyes and take several deep breaths and then let the air out. This will help in the relaxation process. You'll then be asked to **Visualize** some specific setting. You will be asked to imagine your surroundings. You might be asked to imagine that you are lying on a beach. You'll be asked to feel the warmth of the sun on your skin. The hypnotist might actually have the sound of waves washing gently onto the shore playing as recorded sound. If not, this is still all very easy to imagine. As you imagine this, you might hear the sound of seagulls, etc.

As you are imagining this scene, the hypnotist, you'll realize is repeating specific things over and over again. There will be a noticeable **Repetition** of certain specific words and phrases. The hypnotist might mention again how "relaxed" you feel lying there on the beach. Again, your attention might be brought back to how "comfortable" the warmth of the sun feels on your skin. Perhaps you feel a mist of ocean spray that gets carried by the light breeze coming off of the ocean. The waves roll into shore, and a tiny spray of moisture from the white caps gets carried on the breeze and touches lightly on your warm skin. Perhaps you smell the scent of the ocean as the breeze carries this scent to you. You might even taste a bit of dry ocean salt on your upper lip. You then might be asked to notice the tingling sensation as the sun touches on the mist that has landed on your skin. Focus on this feeling. Touch your tongue to your upper lip and taste the salt. Can you taste it? The warmth of the sun dries the mist and the tingling is almost a tickle of exhilaration. And you are sooo **Relaxed** and **Comfortable**. You hear the waves crashing on the shore and the sounds of the seagulls again . . . and you feel the warmth of the sun and you are growing **even more relaxed. More and more relaxed**. Another breeze whisks gently across you, carrying another slight mist. And just behind this breeze is another, lighter one that moves across and whisks the microscopic beads of

the mist away from your body. Again, you feel the warmth of the sun and you are **more and more comfortable**, growing **deeper and deeper Relaxed**. You are going **down** into relaxation, **deeper and deeper down** into **relaxation** . . . Soooo **Relaxed**. You are feeling totally **Relaxed** and **Comfortable**. Soooo completely **Comfortable** and **Relaxed**.
You get the idea:

Relaxation, Visualization, and **Repetition** all play a part in the process.

Focus and Breathing

Two other key factors in hypnosis are Focus and breathing.

Focus plays a major part in the whole hypnotic process. Did you get the urge to lick the salt off your lip earlier? Were you focused on this? You should learn to focus your attention on the sights and sounds of it all.

Focus on the hypnotist's voice as he or she guides you. Notice the individual things that he or she points out or asks you to notice. Focus on the words, on the individual aspects of the whole. And yet, also notice the whole of the scene, letting it wash over you. Become absorbed in the sights, the sounds, the smells. Focus on the fact that you are growing more and more Relaxed. Focus on "Letting Go." Focus on "Relaxing." Your Focus matters. Remember, hypnosis isn't a one-sided game. You are a participant in the process. You **Allow** yourself to Relax. You **Allow** yourself to let go and go deeper and deeper down into relaxation, into trance. You **Allow** yourself to grow more and more comfortable. The hypnotist is only a guide. He or she can't make you go into hypnosis. He or she can only show you the way. You have to want to relax and go deeper into trance. **Relax and Allow** this to happen. Go Deeper and Deeper down. Relax.

And now there is **Breathing.**
Remember how you were asked to take several deep breaths to try and help you relax at the beginning? This was just after you loosened your clothing. Now I want to bring your attention, or Focus, if you will, to breathing.
Let's call it Focused Breathing.
This should be done in a little more depth at the beginning of the relaxation process.

Go ahead, make yourself as comfortable as you can and take a deep breath in through your nose. Hold this breath to the slow count of three, and then let the breath out through your mouth. Push the air all the way out. Let your jaw go slack as you do this. Push the air out. Make sure all of the air is out and hold to the count of three again before taking another big breath in through your nose. Hold again for three and then push the air out again. Again, make sure the air is all the way out of your lungs. Now do it a third time. After you have done this a third time, relax for a minute or so.

After you've rested for a minute or two, try the exercise again. Only this time hold your breath to the count of six and then let the air out, pushing all of the air out of your lungs. Hold for the count of six and then take another big breath in. Remember to keep a slow and steady pace on your count.

Don't rush the count. This is focused, concentrated breathing. If you can't hold for a six count, go back to holding for three and maybe work up to four or five. The idea is to find your ideal rhythm, or pace. Whatever helps to get you relaxed.

Also, sometimes your body is holding stress or tension that you might not be aware of. You might be busy trying to relax into the scene, listening to the voice of the hypnotist, but not achieving the level of relaxation you need or want. Perhaps you are trying too hard, for starters. Maybe, you should just focus on your breathing and simply let the words, or the scene just float or wash over you.

Like I said, however, this breathing exercise should really be done at the beginning. And there is something else that might help.

There is another exercise that is sure to help relax your body. This is a muscle tension and then relaxation process. This is a process of working the muscles to achieve relaxation before proceeding into the hypnotic visualization. Doing this exercise is a sure way to release any tension and then relax you into hypnosis.

Muscle Tense and Release Exercise.

First, start by loosening any clothing, just as you did earlier. Get comfortable.

Now, start at your feet and work up from there. Concentrate on your left foot. Tense the muscles and hold them tight for a couple of seconds. Then let the muscles of the left foot go limp. Try it again.

Next do the same thing with the right foot. And then do the two of them at the same time. Then move to the calves. Do the left, and then the right one. Hold the muscles tense for a few seconds and then release and let the muscles go limp. Next the upper parts of the legs, then the buttocks and the abdomen. And then work the upper part of the body. Hold the muscles tight in your chest and back and then let loose, relax. Do the arms. First each hand and wrist, and then the wrist and forearm. Then move to the upper arms, the triceps and biceps, and then the shoulders. Move to the neck and the face. Tighten and release the muscles all the way up to the top of your head. Hold and then release. Then, hold and maintain your whole body in a tense state for a couple of seconds, every muscle tight and very tense, and then release.

You should try the breathing exercise along with this to really relax. How?

Breath in as you tense the muscles and hold the breath and the muscles to the count of six and then release. As you release the air from your lungs let your muscles go completely limp. Do this. Start with the feet. Tense whatever muscle you are concentrating on as you breath in and hold to the count of six, then let the air out and the muscles relax. Do this all the way up, just like before.

You might try this for a whole week or two, each night, just before going to sleep. Get the practice down. Then, after you have learned how to totally relax your body, you can move on to the visualization part of the exercise.

You can work yourself into a completely re-laxed and trance like state, just by doing this alone.

Two Types of Inductions

1) Guided Visualization
and
2) Rapid Induction

Guided Visualization

Guided Visualization is similar to the beach scene from earlier. The only difference might be that there would be movement involved.

One such scenario might be that you (as subject) might be floating down a river on a raft. You are quite comfortable, with pillows, etc. Again, as with the beach scene, the sun is warm upon your body. There could be other additions of beautiful flowers lining the banks of the river. You might be advised to drag your fingers playfully through the crystal-clear water as you drift along, the raft floating with the moving current. There might be a place where the current spirals in a circular motion, spinning you and the raft in circles before continuing on down the river. And then you might come to a gentler, slower moving current. You maneuver the raft to a bank and then you stand and step off the raft and onto a grassy bank. You then follow a path up and away from the river.

You get the idea here, of course.

The visualization here is similar to the beach visualization. Relaxation is still involved, but you are going someplace, you are moving along for some reason.

So, here you are, walking along a path now. The sun is still warm upon you. You are comfortable, relaxed, walking lazily along with not a care in the world.

And you come upon a building now. The building can be stucco or cement, wood or brick. The details here can be most anything, just something to help add clarity to the visualization

You walk up to a door, open it and enter. Does the door squeak? Is it made of metal? What color is it painted? Is it rusted and old, or is it a new door?

And so you enter the building . . .

Deeper Down

Would you prefer an elevator or would you rather take a stairway?

In the elevator scenario:
You step onto the elevator and the door closes. You push the button to go down. The elevator begins the descent. You look up above the door and see a pointer to the numbers. The arrow pointer is a black wrought iron affair, and the numbers are gathered in a half circle along the top, above the pointer. The pointer is pointing to what number? Twelve? As the elevator descends, watch the numbers and repeat to yourself each number the pointer points to as the elevator moves downward from one floor to the next: Twelve . . . Eleven . . . . Ten . . . Nine . . . Eight . . . Seven . . . Six . . . Five . . .

You are going deeper and deeper down
with each count. The count is slow and me-
thodical. You might hear a whir and feel a
slight jerky vibration as the elevator moves.
You are becoming more and more relaxed
as the elevator moves downward, deeper
and deeper down, more and more relaxed .
. .
Four . . . Three . . . Deeper and deeper
down, more and more relaxed. You are
sooo very relaxed now. Moving deeper and
deeper into sleep, more and more relaxed
Two . . . Deeper and deeper down . . . Deep.
One. So very relaxed.
Do you want to go deeper still?
You exit the elevator and you search, but
there seems to be no elevator on this floor.
Other than the one you just stepped out of.
There is a Stairwell.

The stairway scenario:

You are standing at the top of a stairway leading down. What type of a stairway is it? Is it a circular stairway? Perhaps it simply goes straight down. Picture it in your mind. Can you tell how many steps there are? Looks, you guess, to be about a hundred steps. You don't know for sure, but you start counting as you step onto the first step. You start counting from one hundred. You stop on the first step, the one hundredth step, and take a deep breath. You stop to take a deep breath in and out before stepping down to the next step. One hundred . . . Breathe in and hold the breath and then let the air slowly out and step down to the next step . . .Ninety-nine . . . Breathe in and then out. Step again. Ninety-eight . . .

Ninety-seven . . . Ninety-six . . . Ninety-five . . .

And you might see someone standing at the bottom of the stairway watching you descend. Who might this be? This is probably your conscious mind, watching to make sure that you are safe. You are. You are very safe and comfortable. . .

Ninety-four . . . Breathe in, hold it, and breathe out. Step down Ninety-three . . . Ninety-two . . .

Your conscious mind counts with you as you descend. Or is it your subconscious mind standing down below. No matter. The person standing below looks exactly like you and only has your safety in mind. This you at the bottom of the stairs counts with you. Watch the lips move as you both count along, together as you descend.

You both take a breath in and then let it out.

Ninety-one . . . and again . . . Ninety . . . Eighty-nine . . .

And down you go . . . Deeper and deeper down, both you and your conscious and your subconscious, all of you, moving down, stepping down into the depths of sleep. Down and down. Deeper and deeper. You are becoming even more and more re-laxed the deeper down you go. With each step you are relaxing more and more. Deeper and deeper . . .

Adding Positive Suggestions

With each step down the stairway, as I move down, with each count, I am becom-ing more and more Self Confident . . . Eighty-eight . . . Breathe in, breathe out, more and more Self Confident with each and every step.

With each step down I am feeling Strong and Happy and Confident. I will be more and more Confident in my daily life. More and more Confident and comfortable, here and now, and with each step. I am feeling very Confident that I am becoming more and more happy and am becoming more and more hypnotized with each step. I am a very good hypnotist. I can go into this re-laxed state at any time, becoming more and more relaxed. Easier and easier to go down, deeper and deeper. With each step. Starting with step number Eighty, my Confidence will increase ten-fold on each and every step. I am more and more Self Confident in my daily life and more and more Self Con-fident that I am a good student of Self Hypnosis. I can go into a trance at any time. I am Happy and Confident of this. I feel comfortable and safe, safe and relaxed. With each step . . .

Eighty . . . breathe in and breathe out. More and more Confident. With each breath in I breathe in Confidence and Happiness. Ten times more confident with each step now. More and more confident. More and more relaxed. More and more happy. I look down at myself standing at the bottom of the stairs. I am smiling to myself. I wave. I am happy. We are happy. We are confident. More and more confident and happy.

You can continue on all the way to the bottom of the steps if you so choose. You could have decided in the beginning that there are only ten steps, as opposed to one hundred steps. Then, if you feel the need to go deeper you can simply add or locate another set of steps.
In any case, you will be feeling really good at this point.

You can, at the end of this visualization, find yourself back on the beach from earlier. You are relaxing, listening to the sound

of the waves, hearing the seagulls, feeling the warmth of the sun.
And whenever you feel like, you can stand and stretch and smile, feeling good, sooo good! You can count up to the number three and be wide awake. One . . . Two . . . Three . . . Wide Awake. Now. Feeling re-freshed and relaxed.

So, this is the long, usual induction meth-od. Or, rather, an example of one. You can vary it in many ways. You can add the posi-tive suggestions at any place in the process, so long as you, or the subject are at some level or state of relaxation.

Rapid Induction

So what is Rapid Induction?

While the normal, slower induction method might take anywhere from twenty minutes to an hour, depending, the Rapid Induction technique requires only seconds to achieve a state of hypnosis.

Often, the rapid induction involves a measure of shock and or confusion in the application. Shock and confusion with regard to the subject, I mean. Obviously, the hypnotist knows ahead of time what is happening, what he is going to do to induce hypnosis.

Street hypnotists or performers use this technique all of the time. They have to. It isn't as though the subject or volunteer is going to lie down in the street, or on a busy sidewalk and try and get comfortable while the hypnotist talks them through a guided visualization.

A street hypnotist has to be very experienced and confident to induce a hypnotic trance on the fly (obviously I'm not referring to hypnotizing insects here). The process is a command performance, basically, very similar to a stage hypnotist. Though the fact is, the klieg lights on the stage are helpful in the process. The lights provide for, or induce a sort of disorientation to the volunteers on the stage. And the stage hypnotist also has some sort of music/sound system at his disposal. Not so, the street hypnotist.

The street hypnotist *can* perform the pre-tests on those gathered around, of course, much as the stage hypnotist does.

The Handshake

One of the most common rapid induction techniques is the handshake technique.

The hypnotist reaches for the subject's hand and as the hypnotist grasps the subject's hand he immediately pulls or jerks the subject toward him. The hypnotist, while pulling with his right hand, places his left hand behind the subject's neck and brings the subject's head downward, at the same time commanding the subject to "sleep."

In theory, mentally and literally, the subject is thrown off balance. Being that the handshake is fairly common in western society, everyone is conditioned to it. The subject's mind is conditioned to expect the handshake process to occur as naturally expected. When the hypnotist jerks him forward, there is a jolt to the subject's mental state. This is a totally unexpected move and the subject is mentally (and physically) unprepared for this. A sense of shock and confusion is the result. Within the first second or two, the hypnotist can, if he knows how, convince the subject to go into a trance state. Not only is the subject suddenly mentally thrown off balance and unprepared, he is in fact falling forward, having lost his balance.

I've never used this technique. It is supposed to work. There are several videos and books out there to indicate that it is a legitimate method.

There is also a variation on the handshake:

In this variation, instead of the hypnotist shaking hands, which the subject expects, the hypnotist proceeds to capture the subject's wrist with hypnotist's fingers. He then reaches for the subject's elbow with his (the hypnotist's) left hand and lightly grasps it as well. The hypnotist turns the subject's hand toward the subject and pushes the subject's hand and arm upward toward the subject's face. The palm is pushed to within inches of the subject's face and the subject is told to stare at his own palm.

Again, the shock and confusion of something unexpected is happening. The subject is only mentally thrown off balance in this case. But the conscious mind is confused at this point and the hypnotist can then reach the subconscious and suggest that the subject go deep into a trance.

***

I'm not in any way suggesting or implying that these rapid induction techniques aren't effective. There is evidence/testimony that they do work.

I am only stating here that I have never used them so I do not have any

first-hand knowledge of the proper application of these techniques. I would love to explore these techniques further before trying to give any sort of legitimate instruction.
I have read a couple of books on this subject, however and can describe the process and what I surmise to be going on.

My Take or Experiment on Suggestibility Tests and Rapid Induction

After reading a couple of these "Street Hypnosis" books, I did give some thought as to what sort of pre-hypnotic tests a street hypnotist might could use. The methods would have to be quick and easy, or at least convenient. There are several of the usual methods, of course, that would work. I described one earlier of the arms being used—the suggestion that one arm is being lifted by helium balloons while the other is being heavily weighed down.

Another method would be the suggestion that the subject is sucking on a lemon. The subject's face would then be squinched in a weird way as though he or she is in fact sucking on a lemon.

Often times, the participant is asked to hold their arms out in front of them and clasp their hands together. The participant is then told that the hands are stuck together and he or she should try and pull the hands apart and that they can't. The hands are stuck together, etc.

A variation on this is with the hands clasped together, the participant is asked to stick the index finger of each hand up and hold the index fingers apart from each other. The fingers are not to touch. The participant is then told that the fingers are magnets and the fingers are being pulled together, attracted to one another. The participant is to try and keep the fingers apart. They are told that the magnets are growing stronger and stronger and the force is pulling the two fingers together, etc.

My Thought Experiment

Here was my thought experiment: Being the hypnotist, I would suggest that each individual simply hold his or her index finger before the tip of his or her nose. The index finger would be held just at the tip of the nose, not touching the nose. The subject would then be advised to stare at the finger and to imagine that there is a tiny hand that projects outward from the end of the subject's nose. This tiny hand has an index finger pointing toward the subject's index finger. The subject is not to let the tiny finger of the tiny hand touch his or her index finger. As the subject is imagining the tiny hand, the hand moves toward the subject's finger, the subject is to move his or her finger away. This movement should only be an inch or so. The subject is then asked to push toward the nose with his or her index finger and imagine the tiny hand and tiny finger receding back into the tip of the nose. Again, neither finger touching the other. If the subject's finger actually touches the end of his or her nose, the subject is instructed to relax upon contact. The subject is advised to move the index finger back slowly and watch as the imaginary tiny finger, hand and arm come out again.

The subject should try this once, keeping his gaze fixed on the tip of the nose and the index finger the whole time.

The subject will be advised to slowly pull the index finger back an inch or so, pause, and then move or push it in toward the tip of the nose, imagining the tiny finger and hand backing into the nose tip as the subject's index finger comes in and then coming out of the nose tip as though being drawn out as the subject's index finger is pulled back from the face. Again, we are only talking about a half inch to an inch here.

The subject should back the finger out and then push in again at least five repetitions, moving slowly, with gaze fixed on the tip of the nose and the index finger.

The subject should be advised that if the subject's index finger touches the tiny imaginary index finger, or the tip of the nose, the subject will be instantly relaxed.

Usually, with the first five repetitions of this, without bringing the finger away from the face or nose, the subject, if the gaze has been locked on the tip of the nose and the index finger, should feel a heaviness of the eyes. There should be a slight tension behind the eyes. The eyelids might flutter and the eyes grow heavier with each repetition.

If you experiment with this, you should feel all of this. You should feel the heaviness of the eyelids and the tension behind the eyes.

You should be sitting down when you try this.

First do one set, moving the finger out away from the nose and then in toward the nose, five slow times, fixing the gaze.

Observe the feeling.

Then do this a second time. Do a second set of the five reps, the finger pushing slowly in and then out again.

Imagine that tiny finger being there.

If you don't feel the heaviness after the second set, go on and do a third set of this.

Again, keep your gaze fixed on the end of your nose and the tip of your index finger.

If you are feeling the heaviness and slight tension, you can let your arm move slowly down to rest in your lap. You should be extremely relaxed and your arms should feel very, very heavy now. Imagine trying to move your arms up off of your lap and not being able to do so. You can, of course, if you really try and force the arms up. But you can feel the heaviness and you might not have any desire to actually lift your heavy arms.
Your eyelids might feel so heavy and you might not be able to open your eyes. Go ahead and try . . . Again, if you really push, you will be able to, but the desire to open your eyes probably isn't very strong.

You can go Deeper and Deeper down if you wish. You can sit still and feel this state, experience this relaxed state.

Your eyes should be closed and your arms heavy in your lap.

If you've never experienced this before, this is what the hypnotic trance state feels like.

This medium to heavy trance state was achieved in just a couple of minutes.

Know that you will be able to come up out of this state by just telling yourself to wake up. You can again count up from one to three and then say "Wake Up," or "I now Wake Up," and you will awaken. Or, "I Will Awaken. Now."

When you wake up you might be aware of feeling a little groggy. This is ok. It will pass. Close your eyes again and say something like "I feel refreshed and wide awake." And open your eyes.

***

As you might imagine, since I was merely trying to think of a good quick pre-test for possible hypnotic subjects, I was quite surprised when I went deeply into a trance state almost immediately.

So, this turned out to be a rather quick induction method in and of itself.

Thinking about it now, I should have realized that it would be an induction, because it uses one of the tried-and-true methods that have been used for inducing hypnosis for centuries. What was that?

Eye Fixation.

When you affixed your gaze on the tip of your nose and your index finger and held it there, that—as eye fixation does—put a strain on your eyes. This strain causes your eyes to grow tired. The same thing happens when you try and roll your eyes back up into your head, to the point where just your sclera (the whites of your eyes) is showing. This also was a method used in the past to see if the subject could go into trance. If the subject was showing a good bit of the whites of the eyes when the hypnotist raised the lids to check, Yep, that subject was most likely in a trance state.

Now, please do not try and roll your eyes back into your head. Especially

WARNING

if you suffer from epilepsy, or have trouble playing video games for long periods of time. If you have any sort of disability in this regard, don't even try the finger technique. You should NOT be participating in any hypnosis exercises at all.

Now, having said this, if you did the experiment and all was fine, I would suggest that you play around with taking yourself deeper once you are under, or in trance. If you were able to feel what I described earlier, then you know what I am talking about here. Here is how I took it further. I'll give you an example of how I incorporated a relaxation technique into the finger/nose induction method.

I call the whole method the Hummingbird Induction. It will become obvious to you why I call it that in a minute. And, of course, this sounds a lot better than the finger/nose technique.

Once I was under, I used a little guided visualization to take myself further down. I started by suggesting to myself that I could see (even though my eyes were closed) feathers floating downward. I imagined this. First, I pictured one or two feathers floating to the ground. They floated slowly, back and forth, slowly down, back and forth. I repeated this. I started out with one or two white feathers, and then gray and black ones. And then I imagined colored ones: orange and purple and yellow . . . and they all floated back and forth as they moved down toward the ground. I repeated "back and forth," "downward," "I am floating down deeper into relaxation, becoming more and more relaxed." I made sure I was totally relaxed and then I could imagine hearing a sort of buzzing or humming sound, coming from up toward my head. The sound was coming from six to eight inches from my face. Then I saw it (through my closed eyes, in my imagination), a hummingbird. It was hovering there, looking at me. I watched him, and he was watching me. I stared at him and he stared back. He was hovered there staring at me, just inches from my face. His wings were moving rapidly and there was a humming sound. Then as I watched, he still hovered, but was moving backward, slowly. As he was moving backward, still staring at me, I was imagining him pulling me deeper and deeper into relaxation. The further away he moved, the more relaxed I became. Then he moved to his left. I could see him hovering there for a second. And just before he moved, the word Relax appeared. Relax just hung in the air. The humming bird moved to his right and the word

Relax crumbled to pieces and disappeared. But the word Relax appeared where the bird was now hovering, to the right. Relax. The bird moved again to the left and the same thing happened, where he had previously been the word Relax crumbled and disappeared. Multi colored letters, just like the feathers had been. Now, the feathers had nothing to do with the humming bird, they were just random, independent imaginings. And the hummingbird still watched me. He still zigged and zagged, hovering in various spots. And he slowly backed up and away, pulling me deeper and deeper into relaxation. And I continued to watch him, following into the distance, growing more and more relaxed. Eventually, he moved back so far that he dwindled to a mere speck and then disappeared. Puff, he was gone. And I was totally relaxed.

And the thought hit me that I could practice this to the point that I could just imagine this hummingbird and be immediately in a state of trance. I would have to practice this. I could give myself the suggestion that this would happen, that any time I wanted to achieve this state all I had to do was see the hummingbird suspended there a foot or so from my face.

This wasn't something that would be an everyday happening, so I would be safe imagining it and using it.

I've never, in fact had a hummingbird suspended in mid air directly in front of my face. I've seen them, yes, but never had them that close, right up front and center. So, great, I can use this. All I have to do is imagine the hummingbird hovering there staring at me.

You can imagine anything and use it. The tiny finger coming out of the tip of the nose was sort of bizarre, wasn't it? I suppose you could imagine bubble gum instead of the tiny hand. You would pull the bubble gum, stretching it as you move the finger away and then the gum would recede back into the tip of the nose as the index finger comes toward the nose tip.

It is all crazy, I know. If you want, as I discovered later, imagine that you have wires or strings extending from the center of the lower part of your upper eyelids (at the middle of your lashes) running alongside your nose and attached to your index finger. And as you pull your finger away from the end of your nose (never more than half an inch, remember) these strings or wires are gently tugging your eyelids down into the closed position. This is what I did.

And, I even took things further, realizing after experimentation, that I could, while lying in bed in the dark (not being able to see my finger) I could achieve the same result. The trick was to still be holding my eyes in the position of staring at my finger and the end of my nose and imagining both.

You can use your imagination in all kinds of ways to induce hypnosis. In fact, I have a whole book on that subject:

Here there be Tygers: Hypnosis through the Imagination.

Let's talk more about

Eye Fixation

as it relates to Hypnosis.

You can sit quietly and gaze at an object (pretty much any object, the brighter the object the better) fixedly for a short period of time and induce a trance.

The object you fix your gaze on can be a stationary object or it can be a moving object.

Remember the old movie where the evil hypnotist has the subject (victim in this case) stare fixedly into his eyes. Yes, that works, to a degree. You probably tried the staring contest when you were a kid. Your eyes want to blink. The eyes grow tired from the stress and holding them open causes a dryness. You want to alleviate the dryness by blinking to moisten the eye. And if you hold the eyes open long enough, they do start to "water" on their own.

Remember the pendulum. You've also seen those movies, right? The hypnotist (not necessarily evil, of course)

swinging the pendulum back and fort
in front of the subject.

You not only have the pendulum re-
flecting the light as it swings back and
forth, but the swinging back and forth
is soothing, the undulating back and
forth as your gaze follows. And note
how the hypnotist is holding the pendulum up and above eye level. The
subject's eyes are looking upward and
the gaze is locked on the pendulum.
Remember me mentioning the rolling
of the eyes up and back. The strain of
the eyes in any position is effective for
creating a tiredness. When our gaze
was affixed to the finger at the end of
the nose, our eyes were almost
crossed. A definite strain, prompting
a sense of tiredness; the heavy eyelids

and pressure behind the eyes resulting in a trance.

There is the psychedelic disc, spinning or not. If you stare at it for any length of time you will achieve results. Your eyes will grow tired and you can and should move into a trance.

You can sit in a darkened room and stare at a lighted candle. This works, but I would use caution. Obviously, you don't want to fall asleep while a candle is burning, unless you have it in a candle holder with glass sides.

You can stare at most any object. It is the fixation of the gaze that does the trick. A doorknob might work, even. Though it is often best to use something bright and shiny.

How about a mirror?

Yes, a mirror is excellent. You have to have patience. You can sit or stand in front of the mirror and stare into your own eyes, or at some small bright object. Or, you can affix the psychedelic disc to the mirror. The easiest and most convenient approach is to simply stare into your own eyes.

Claude M. Bristol discusses what he calls the mirror technique in his book, *The Magic of Believing*. He suggests that you stand with your shoulders back and your chest out and then take a deep breath in while staring into your eyes. Then at this point you use positive affirmations, etc. You allow yourself to believe that you will achieve whatever it is that you want to achieve. You make a mental picture of the thing happening and believe that it will happen.

Very similar to hypnosis, no?

You affix your gaze on something— your own eyes. You breathe in and out to become relaxed. At this point you might be attempted to let your mind wander to other things, such as whether or not it is time for a haircut, etc. Don't let this happen. If you can settle in and concentrate on your breathing and keep your gaze focused, you should be able to achieve this.

Do as we discussed earlier with your breathing: Breathe in and hold to a count of six. Or you might breathe in to the count of six and then hold for a count of three and breathe out again, pushing all the air out to the count of six. Do this about three times, and then . . .

Start counting down from one hundred, and between the count of one hundred and ninety-nine breathe in and hold the breath for three, letting the air out as you say ninety-nine. And do this again. Breathe in and say ninety-eight, hold the breath and let it out. After a few minutes, you should be a little more focused and relaxed. Keep your gaze fixed.

You might sort of defocus your eyes a little, just let this happen as you imagine a light emanating around the contours of your body. Imagine the light growing. You can perhaps coordinate this along with your breath. Repeat mentally that you are becoming more and more Relaxed and going Deeper and Deeper Down . . . and actually feel this happening. You can tell yourself that you become better and better at going into trance each time you do this. Tell yourself that you become better and better at hypnosis each and every day.

Of course, you should have in mind some sort of goal you are trying to achieve. You should have this goal or trait honed down to one or two sentences, something that can be written on a 3 x 5 card and memorized. Perhaps your intent is to become more confident, as in the example earlier. Maybe there is some other trait you want to work on.

Initially, you can just concentrate on relaxing, and imagine the light emanating from your body. I would be surprised if after a few days of this some friend or acquaintance doesn't remark that you "seem different," or that there is something about you, "a certain glow." Perhaps a "glow of confidence."

Don't be afraid to experiment. Start with some small thing you want to change, some trait you want to acquire. Work on this every day, make it a habit. Try this for a couple of weeks. Every day. And see if there is a change. You should feel better. Perhaps you do nothing more than use the old Emile Coué phrase:

"Day by day, in every way, I am getting better and better."

Use the Dial Technique

As you are standing there before the mirror, in a very relaxed and confident trance, sense how you feel. Imagine a scale from one to ten (ten being high and one being low). How do you feel? Play with this. Imagine what a level two would feel like. Then imagine what level five would be. Relate this to the glow that you imagine emanating from your body. Picture a dial in your mind with the numbers around it. You turn the dial up and watch the light around your body getting brighter and growing outward, shining out from around you. See how bright that glow is at level ten. After you have worked on this for a while, you will be more in control during the day. You can just imagine this dial and turn the dial to whatever level you need. Turn the dial up when you need to be "On." It is a system of projection.

Play around, but don't strain or struggle. Don't try to "will" this. This is a Visualization. Use your imagination. It has been said that when the will and the imagination are in competition, the imagination always wins!

"Our actions spring not from our will, but from our Imagination." –Emile Coué

Suggestion and Auto Suggestion

Hypnosis is all about suggestion, and or auto suggestion. How the suggestion is presented is important. How do you talk to yourself? Do you demand things of yourself? Do you command yourself? Or, do you merely state that it is ok to allow yourself to do a thing?

Often times someone will not go into hypnosis because there is no rapport between the hypnotist and the subject.

Perhaps the hypnotist is a commanding presence, and *demands* that you go into hypnosis. But suppose you, as subject, don't really feel any respect for this person. It might be that you don't care much for authority figures, or there might simply be something about this particular individual that rubs you the wrong way. If this is the case, you can try all you want, but you probably won't go under unless this changes. Perhaps it never will. Find someone else (speaking here of therapy sessions, not with/of the street hypnotist).

Don't get me wrong. A hypnotist is often firm and commands you while you are in a trance. There is a confidence that the hypnotist must project. And, if this hypnotist has a lot of experience, he might know exactly what he is doing and know that this works. It will be ok to follow along and "let go."

The hypnotist must have confidence in himself. You must have confidence in him or her. But most of all, you must have confidence that you will relax and achieve the trance state. Remember that when it comes down to it, all hypnosis is self-hypnosis. You have to play along, be compliant, and want to achieve the relaxed state.

If you are fighting going into hypnosis, then there is something wrong. Even if you think you want to go under, something is holding you back. Maybe it is a case of you not fully trusting anyone. Maybe you feel that you will be in a vulnerable state when you are under hypnosis. Technically you are correct, as you will be in a highly suggestible state. But remember that no one can make you do something you do not want to do. But it does boil down to trust. How trusting *are* you? Is it that you don't trust the individual hypnotist, or are you still afraid of hypnosis itself? Remember the stairs in the earlier visualization. Remember that you imagined your conscious mind standing at the bottom of the stairs, watching? The idea was that your conscious mind is standing guard. Your conscious mind is protecting you and at the same time, often, standing in the way, blocking you from achieving hypnosis.

The idea of that particular visualization is that your conscious mind follows along, also counting, also becoming more and more relaxed. Also becoming compliant, becoming hypnotized.

If this doesn't work, and you are not comfortable with someone else hypnotizing you, the beauty is that after reading this book you should be able to do Self-hypnosis.

And then, if the conscious mind is still blocking you, observe how you try and convince yourself. Do you command yourself?

Often it might work better if you tell yourself that it is ok to *allow* yourself to relax. Sometimes it is all in the

wording, the conversational approach.

Also, I don't know if you noticed that while we were doing the visualization, the pronouns changed back and forth. Sometimes I would be using the 'you' and sometimes I would switch things as though you were telling yourself. I would suggest or imply that you were the one suggesting, hence the 'I' at times. And then, I believe I used 'we' at times also.

Often confusion works. Remember the handshake in the rapid induction technique. When someone reaches to shake your hand, your mind perceives that is what is going to happen. Your mind is conditioned to expect that

that is what is going to happen. But then that doesn't happen. Confusion. There is also conversational confusion. I'm not going to cover it here, but a few years ago, (and possibly still, mainly due to the sudden popularity of NLP) "Covert," or "Indirect" hypnosis was all the rage.

I believe I might have mentioned earlier that sometimes metaphors, or stories are used to achieve results. The late Dr. Milton Erickson was a master of the indirect technique. Often it would be through the use of confusing language or speech patterns.

There are plenty of books on the subject and there are a ton of resources and information on Dr. Erickson. He was a pioneer in the field and has become sort of a God like figure when it comes to hypnosis.

In any case, getting back to the fact that your subconscious (or even your conscious mind) is blocking you from achieving results . . . when you are at home, alone, practicing self-hypnosis, you should feel more comfortable. Perhaps, as you do the visualization where you are going down the stairs, when you reach the bottom of the stairs you can picture yourself shaking hands with your subconscious (or conscious) self. You might even put your arm around 'your' shoulders when you meet. The two of you need to work together. There needs to be trust. Think of the power you will have when you work together. Perhaps there is some truth to the suggestion of "me, myself, and I." There is the you that is observing all of this. This 'you' is stepping into the role of conscious you one minute and then the subconscious you the next. How's that for confusion?

Association and Repetition

You probably have something, some object, in your life that whenever you look at it you are reminded of someone you once knew. Perhaps the object was a gift from someone. An example might be a quilt that your grandmother made. Perhaps there is a scent, whether it be perfume or cologne, or the smell of brewing coffee that automatically *triggers* certain thoughts of a time, place or person, etc.

We all have these "triggers." Two or more things become associated in our mind. Often there is a strong emotion involved. You might have been bitten by a particular breed of dog when you were a child, and now, years later, if you see a dog of this breed a sense of fear washes over you. This fear might have receded a little over the years, but it is still there. Seeing the dog triggers the feeling. Why? Well, getting bit by a dog, especially as a child, is more likely than not to be a traumatic event. The feelings associated with the event are powerful. Perhaps you go to a hypnotist to relieve or remove this association. This associative technique is often used in hypnosis as well as in memory enhancement programs. In memorizing something, perhaps a word, you continually repeat, or associate the word with the definition of the word to get it to stick in your mind.

If you were an NLP (neuro-linguistic programming) practitioner, or instructor, you might use this technique and call it "anchoring." An object might become an anchor, where the instructor repeatedly works to associate the object with a certain state or feeling. The instructor would repeatedly work the individual into a heightened positive state and associate the object, or a certain action (such as the student touching two fingers of one hand together) to anchor the two.

A stage hypnotist might simply suggest to a hypnotized participant on stage that when he or she awakens (which would make this a post hyp-notic suggestion) the person next to this participant smells extremely good, or bad. This makes for a funny routine, as often enough the partici-pant buries his or her nose in the clothing of the person next to them while that person wonders what is happening and tries moving away. The stage hypnotist hasn't repetitively "anchored" this association in the participant's mind, though he might have suggested it a couple of times to the hypnotized individual. This would be a short-term effect or association, which the hypnotist would reverse (hopefully) before the participant leaves the stage.

You can use this. You can choose a certain visualization, or a certain image within that visualization and repeatedly anchor it in so that when you think of this item or image, you will go immediately into trance. I do this with the hummingbird image from my earlier experiment. All I have to do is imagine a hummingbird hovering six to twelve inches from my face and I go into a light trance state. From there, I can go deeper if I so choose.

The more you practice hypnosis, along with giving yourself the suggestion that you can achieve the state faster and faster each time, the easier the process will become.

Use the technique of associating something with the trance state, repeating the process to strengthen the connection, over and over.

Of course, you would not want to do this with an object or situation that is common in everyday life. You wouldn't want to get triggered automatically at an inopportune time. For instance, you wouldn't want to associate the ringing of a bell, to trigger yourself. You might be in your boss's office, talking to him and have his phone ring. That might only be good if you associate the ring with a suggestion of you becoming more relaxed and confident. But overall, it's best to be careful about such things.

There is an old episode of *The Dick Van Dyke Show*, where Dick accidentally or indirectly becomes hypnotized to go into a drunken state every time a bell rings. There is a scene where he is going in and out of this state on his way to answering the telephone. The first ring, he is drunk, the second ring sobers him up, but as he is on his way to answer the phone it rings a third time . . .

Yes, hummingbirds exist. However, I don't see them every day. And the chances of one hovering six inches from my face and staring at me, thus triggering a trance, is highly remote. So, I feel pretty safe using this image.

Setting up to do Self Hypnosis at home.

You'll need a few things here:
Some sort of recording device.
Audio editing software.
A script of sorts, part of which lays out the guided visuals and the also the affirmations or positive changes you wish to make.

***

I used to record things old school. I would use an old-fashioned microphone and record onto a tape recorder. Then I would use an audio cable (plugged from the headphone jack of the tape recorder/player to the microphone jack of the computer) to feed the playing tape into the computer; and then edit the whole in audio editing software (Magix Audio Cleaning Lab 2004). Then I would burn the edited audio file to CD and play in a CD player with headphones at night, just before going to sleep. Today there are quite a few different options. You can probably just record directly to your cell phone and then listen straight from there whenever you want.

If you want to play around, however, and edit things, there are at least two different *free* audio editing programs: Audacity and Garage Band. I've played with Audacity a little bit, but I've never used Garage Band.

I have tried a lot of different ways to record. I've used old empty paper towel or toilet paper rolls to shield the microphone from outside noise. I would take the microphone and stick it snugly into one end of the roll and speak into the other end. I have also tried coffee cans, laying the mic in the bottom of the can and then putting my face up to the opening and speaking into it. I've used both the metal and the plastic cans for this. The trick is to get creative. There are so many ways to use sound.

I'm guessing you should be able to prop your cell phone in the bottom of a can if you want to try that. The main thing is to block out surrounding noise as much as possible. You know, each room has an acoustic presence, depending. Step into the shower and try recording in there.

You can do a ton of different things with editing software. Don't be afraid to play and experiment. You can add background tracks of anything from waves crashing on the shore to pattering rain, etc. There are a lot of free sound effects out there. Or simply record your own effects.

Once you decide how you are going to record things, then design your script. The script doesn't have to be anything fancy. Just lay out a guided visualization. A path, if you will. Then add positive affirmations or commands to stop smoking, or commands to lose weight, or whatever. The key to these commands, however, is to make sure you think the commands through and word them correctly.

For instance, if you are trying to lose weight you don't want to suggest that you suddenly have no taste for food. Suppose it took, and you suddenly, from then on could not or would not eat. Obviously, you have to eat to live. You might try suggesting that you eat small portions of food and yet feel just as full as when you had eaten the larger portions.

With cigarettes you can suggest that each puff or drag on a cigarette that you take will taste worse and worse until you lose all desire for smoking. Think of some taste that would be absolutely awful to you. I've read of people suggesting that each puff tastes like burnt, or burning rubber. You might think of some food you absolutely hate and suggest that the cigarette tastes like that food.

The trick to all of this working is that you have to actually, really want to quit smoking in the first place.

The reason I suggest that you be careful how you word your script is that your mind, the subconscious mind anyway can't tell the difference when it comes down to it between a thought that is real or one that is imagined. What I mean to say is that, using the sucking on a lemon analogy, whether you are actually sucking on a real lemon or just imagining that you are sucking on a lemon, the effect is the same. You get the sour reaction.

Whether you have the weights on one arm pushing or pulling it down, and helium filled balloons attached to the other arm pulling it up doesn't matter. The subconscious mind is going to accept the suggestion as real, if you imagine it clearly enough, just as if the situation is real. Your subconscious mind can't distinguish the difference. It doesn't care. The subconscious simply accepts. You picture something in your mind, focus on that picture, the mind sees it. If that same item is real and actually in front of you, your eyes see it and it too registers in your mind in the same way. If you picture a pink elephant in your mind, it doesn't matter if there is a real pink elephant standing in front of you or not. Your conscious mind knows the difference. Your conscious mind will be saying "Hey, there is no such thing." Your conscious mind is logical. Your subconscious mind is not logical. Your conscious mind questions things based on your life experience, etc. Your subconscious mind simply accepts what is presented to it.

Sorry to keep beating you over the head with this, but it is important.

As an example of something that really bothers me:

"Money doesn't grow on trees" vs "Money grows on trees."

We all know that money, in fact, doesn't grow on trees. This is a logical statement that you probably heard when you were a child. I know I did. Every time I asked my mother if she could buy me something that was expensive (usually something I didn't actually need), she would make the statement "Money doesn't grow on trees." Aside from being technically accurate, there was the meaning that has been attached to this statement: "We don't have money to waste on extraneous items." Or something similar to this.

So, being familiar with this statement, and knowing that the subconscious mind simply accepts statements presented to it, I was really surprised by a suggestion on a current "Abundance/Manifestation" recording that I was listening to recently (Yes, I like to see what's out there—curious to check out suggestions and affirmations being used). Here is the suggestion: "Money *does* grow on trees!"

Now I realize that the person who decided to use this statement is just trying to counteract the negative statement that we have been programmed with. But, I'm thinking, this statement isn't accurate (which it isn't). I'm thinking, if I'm in a highly suggestible state or trance and I hear this "money *does* grow on trees" statement, what is to keep me from believing it to the extent that I decide that if I need money all I have to do is pluck it from the trees all around in my yard? This is absurd, of course. All the same, I always imagine myself standing at the edge of my driveway and plucking at the leaves of the several trees that are there. I imagine my next-door neighbor walking over and asking me what I am doing, to which I respond, "I'm just gathering together some money because I'm going to go to the grocery store."

Like I said, this is absurd, and I'm exaggerating things quite a bit. But you get my point, right? This is something a stage hypnotist might use. The stage hypnotist might suggest to a hypnotized participant on stage that there is a tree on stage and the participant is to pluck as much money as he or she can from this tree. Or, to suggest the opposite of this—that the participant is to open his or her wallet or pocket book to find nothing but leaves and he or she is to treat them as such. The participant would probably be plucking these "leaves" from the wallet and tossing them to the floor of the stage. Okay, so you understand my point: The subconscious is not very discerning when it comes down to it, especially when suggestions are given while the individual is in a trance state.

So, you must word your script accordingly.

If you don't want to make up your own scripts, there are pre-made scripts on the market, in book form, for quitting smoking and for weight loss.

You can just do the relaxation sugges-tions and the visualizations and then incorporate the anti-smoking or weight loss script as necessary.

Write your script for all of it down on a piece of paper, or three by five cards and commit it to memory before re-cording it. It doesn't have to be exact, especially the visualization and relax-ation part. The affirmations, or sug-gestions pertaining to your objective, whether it be quitting smoking or weight loss, **Do** need to be exact, however.

Work on this in front of the mirror, memorizing all of it. This is no differ-ent than when you were in school and had to memorize a speech that you would then later give in class. The only difference is that this "speech" you are going to record for your own benefit, to be read to you when you are nice and relaxed and in a trance state. It is important to remember that hypnosis takes practice. You probably won't notice anything happening, or any big changes right off the bat. It might take a while. Or, you might find that it works right away (lucky you), but then seems to fade days or weeks later and you fall back to old habits as though you had never tried to change. Just listen to the recording again. Repetition is key. Don't sweat it. There have been, according to the literature, post hypnotic suggestions that have lasted for a year or more. So who knows? I don't believe any hypnotherapist has just repeatedly checked for years on end whether a suggestion held. And, individuals are different, as with anything else. You might be better at sports, scoring goals more consistently than a friend who has practiced more often. Or perhaps you are more focused when you concentrate and have better study habits generally (improving study habits is another reason to try hypnosis). It all varies depending on the person. Keep working at it and don't stress about it. As you know **Relaxation** is key.

I have a hypnosis recording that I have been listening to off and on for years. This isn't one I recorded myself. The recording is somewhat general, but there is a statement that is helpful, since I am a writer: "Your mind is a great reservoir of creative ideas." This seems to help.

When I first started listening, I went into the process thinking that I would just relax and listen and not worry about whether I got results or not. The relaxation part on this recording is good, with a good guided visualization. Sometimes I find my mind wandering and I'm not really paying attention. Other times I just try and "let go" and see how relaxed I can become; see how deep into relaxation I can go.

My theory is that if it isn't working, then I am no worse off than when I started listening.

Does it work?

I know that every time I sit down to write, ideas always come.

Is this because I am an experienced writer and have been writing for quite a few years now, or is it because of the hypnosis recording?

Perhaps some of both.

Do I listen every night? No. Used to be I only listened one night a week. For some reason, if I listened two nights in a row, I seemed to have a small headache and would want to sleep a lot the following few days. I would feel groggy. Some hypnotists talk about a "hypnosis hangover." I don't know if that's what it was. I just kept it at once a week for a long while. Occasionally, I would listen two nights a week. I would just space the two nights out.

Lately I've been listening for quite a few nights in a row, just to see. The most I've done is probably a week and a half at a time before there is a night that I lie down and think about putting on the headphones and then starting the CD player (yes, I'm still doing things the old-fashioned way) and then fall asleep before I actually do so.

With you it will probably be your phone and earbuds rather than headphones.

Speaking of which, you should definitely use the buds or headphones rather than just playing through speakers in the room. The phones/buds help to tune out other noises or distractions. They work better.

Some Final Thoughts

You can look at this book as a sort of *preconditioning tool*. The information presented within these pages is meant to be instructive and informative. And yet, this is only a start. As with anything else you learn, you'll have to put this information to use for it to be valuable for you.

There is a reason I just used the term(s) "Preconditioning tool." Keep this in mind and I will eventually explain what I mean by this.

We all go through life with preconceived notions about things. It is unfortunate that in the case of hypnosis most people come to the subject with preconceived notions, ideas or impressions of something mysterious and/or magical. This mystery and magic might be a little exciting, right? And yet, the ideas of mystery and magic imply that hypnosis is something beyond our understanding. Or, even worse, these preconceived ideas, along with the mistaken idea that the hypnotist has some sort of magical power over the person being hypnotized often lead us to be fearful. If there is fear, then we want to stay away from whatever might be causing us to be fearful. This makes sense, of course. Take someone who had lived four or five hundred years ago. If this person were to be brought into our world today, they would be fearful. All of todays technology that we in our everyday lives take very much for granted, all of this would be magical and mystical to this person. All of these things: Microwaves, cell phones, movies, electric light, automobiles, etc. would instill fear, if not outright horror in this person. Why? Because they don't understand. These technological marvels are merely tools to help us get through our lives on a daily basis. We *understand* how these tools work, so we don't fear them. We use these tools.

Well, that is all hypnosis is, a tool. This is important to keep in mind: HYPNOSIS is a tool! That's it, that's all it is. Hypnosis has been studied for centuries. Use of it has been widespread. The subject is, overall, well understood. Granted, each person might experience hypnosis a little differently. The experience is subjective. You experience it differently due to thoughts and feelings that you have within you. Whatever notions you have, or experiences you have experienced as an individual are all floating around in your mind, within your subconscious. This is the only difference. But—and this is key—the *tool* of hypnosis is the same. The techniques or methods that each hypnotist uses might vary a little. The visualizations used might be a little different. But, overall, all of the hypnotists start from the same place, the same foundation. They all use the same tool. And you can use this tool also, to effect positive change in your life, now that you understand what hypnosis is all about.

Now, getting back to the idea of this book being a preconditioning tool. Remember what I've said about how you (or *we*, because I also came into the study of the subject with many of the same notions as you) come into the study of hypnosis with preconceived ideas? You have been *conditioned* to have or believe these ideas. This conditioning might not have been overtly intentional. It wasn't. The misunderstanding of hypnosis and what hypnosis is all about is the problem. You are probably familiar with the Russian scientist Pavlov and his experiments with dogs. Pavlov conditioned his dogs to the point where they would salivate at the ringing of a bell. He conditioned the dogs to associate feeding time with the ringing of the bell. And so, the dogs inevitably began to salivate at the ringing of the bell due to anticipatory thoughts of food.

Most people hear the word hypnosis and they associate mystery and magic with the word due to conditioning. This book is a preconditioning tool in the sense that it will help you begin to change your thoughts on what hypnosis is all about. You will become more informed as you read the information herein. You will come to know that hypnosis isn't some magical or mystical thing. You will be *preconditioned,* as this book and the information it contains is only the beginning. The old conditioning will fall away as you begin to think about hypnosis in a new way.

Once you have gone through the pre-conditioning phase of learning and absorbing the information, then you can begin conditioning yourself to practice hypnosis on a regular basis. Once you have decided on your induction method and visualizations, and figure out what works best for putting yourself into the trance state, you can then (with practice) condition yourself to go into trance more quickly and more deeply each time.

As a side note, as I mentioned earlier, I have conditioned myself to just imagine a hummingbird floating a foot or so from my face to become relaxed. Also, I can now just imagine my index finger at or near the end of my nose to induce a trance. I no longer have to physically perform the act (as long as I hold my eyes in the proper position that they would be in if I were staring at the finger).

I'm not saying that you have to use this method exactly as I do. I have a multitude of varying methods and visualizations. With practice and conditioning, you can achieve hypnosis in a short time.

Once you have figured out your plan, your visualizations and induction method, etc., you can add in your positive affirmations or statements to achieve whatever you have in mind. You can even add the positive suggestion that you "will achieve hypnosis ten times faster each time you hypnotize yourself." You "will go deeper and deeper with each session."

Of course, if you are recording your own voice and using the recording to hypnotize yourself, you would switch the pronoun from "you" to "I," as in "I will go deeper and deeper . . ."

And don't "sweat" whether the positive information or suggestions are "going in." What I mean by this is that you do not tense up or try really hard—or worry about this. Just relax and eventually you will get results. You could even add in a positive suggestion that you/I "can focus on the suggestions directly, or not. Even if your (or my) mind wanders it doesn't matter, the suggestions will still work because your (or my) subconscious mind is listening and absorbing these suggestions."

Playing with Time

You can get really creative in playing with time and hypnosis. I'm sure you've heard the expression "Time flies when you're having fun." Want to slow it down? Have you ever wished to make the workday seem to go by faster? You can do this, by just giving yourself the suggestion that it will seem to go by faster. Just make sure to tell yourself that you will still manage to get all of your work done.

I haven't played with this a lot, but this area does fascinate me and I hope to experiment a little more in the future.

In the book, *The Complete Guide to Hypnosis*, by Leslie M. LeCron, the author relates the story of a man who hypnotized his ten-year old son and gave him the suggestion that he should replay in his mind the movie that the father and son had watched together a few days earlier. The son was advised to watch the two-hour movie at a fast speed, or in a short-ened time (ten minutes, I believe). While the child was under, his right arm rapidly moved up and down, from his lap to his face and back to his lap. When the father awakened his son, he asked what the son was doing. The son stated that he had been eat-ing popcorn, just as he had when the two had watched the movie in the theater.

This was funny and interesting. Children between certain ages (age seven and thirteen) make the best hypnotic subjects.

A good book, though very dry and clinical, on the subject of experimenting with time and hypnosis is *Time Distortion in Hypnosis: An Experimental and Clinical Investigation (Second Edition)*, by Linn F. Cooper, M.D. & Milton H. Erickson, M.D.. My only experimentation on the subject has been indirectly. I used the Dial Technique that I have described earlier in relation to my own actions. I imagined the dial, and gave myself the suggestion that when I turned the dial up to a higher number, I would be more energized and move more quickly, performing whatever actions I happened to be doing at a much faster pace. Performing the task, while awake, I imagined the dial with a range from 1-10 and imagined myself turning the dial up from say 4 to 6 or 8. The result was successful, I might add.

Hypnosis without hypnosis?

There is an idea floating around in certain circles that hypnosis itself doesn't exist. The idea is that we are in varying trance states all day long every day, all of our lives. You don't have to be "put into" hypnosis because you are already *there* is the idea. Think about this for a minute. Think about your own particular everyday life.

You are constantly being bombarded with an onslaught of information. There are all kinds of things going on around you all of the time. You can not deal with everything at once. This would be impossible. You would suffer from information overload. One might say that this would fry your brain and completely exhaust your body. You couldn't handle everything. And so, your body/mind is set up to tune some things out while focusing on other things.

Think about being in a grocery store. You are shopping for groceries. There you are pushing your cart, figuring out what you need and where that item is located in the store, etc. All the while there are people moving all around you doing the same thing. Visually, you are taking in and processing all of the colors, objects on the shelves and prices of everything. There are the signs above the aisles, the colorful fruits and vegetables that are on the shelves in one area of the store. There is the bright and bold packaging of other items. You are visually searching for what you need, for your familiar items, the items on your grocery list. Visually, also, you are taking in all of the movements of the other individuals, where they are at, where they are going, etc. Some of this you absorb naturally. You sense which direction another person is going in and you try to stay out of each other's way. Think about the auditory side of things. There are conversations going on all around you, all over the store. You can hear the conversation of two neighbors or acquaintances who have just run into each other the next aisle over. You can hear the music coming over the speakers, which is interrupted with announcements from management. You hear the thump of a cart hitting the push double doors as an employee comes from a back room with more inventory to be put out on shelves. You are hearing dings and buzzes and whirs and bumps and perhaps a crash of something getting knocked over. You are hearing other customers asking employees where a particular item is located, or whether an item will be back in stock soon.

All of this is going on all around you, all over the store. You cannot possibly take it all in. There is no need.

You aren't focused on everything. Perhaps you focus on a sound, or a conversation momentarily, but you then focus again on your list. Your conscious mind is only focused on your shopping list as that is what is important. Meanwhile, your subconscious is sorting through all the rest of the sounds and sights, constantly taking things in. You are no longer listening to the two neighbors on the next aisle. However, suppose one of the two individuals mentions something they have come to the store to purchase, and you suddenly find that your attention is back on the conversation—you tune in and hear mention of that item, why? Well, perhaps you had thought of the same item earlier, decided you needed it, but were busy with something else at the time you thought of it. Then later on when you were creating your grocery list, you forgot to add it to your list. Now you add it, thankful that your subconscious brought the conversation back into focus and drew your conscious mind to it.

Hours later, well after you have left the store, you realize that you have a certain song playing in the back of your mind. Why? Where had you heard it last? Had that song been playing on the music system of the grocery store? Or was it the background music of a commercial that you had seen on T.V. after you got home?

Or, maybe you are in the kitchen putting the groceries up and spy one of your children's school backpacks sitting on the kitchen table. You suddenly remember the child asking you the night before whether you could pick up something they need for an upcoming school project . . . You had forgotten to make this second stop to pick up the needed items. You meant to, but . . .

OK, so you get my point here, of course. Your mind (both consciously and subconsciously) is continually sorting through all of the information you are being bombarded with. Your focus continues to shift from one thing to another.

To continue with the example, you might have a conversation that you had at work playing in the back of your mind while you are busy putting up the groceries, and you are wondering why something about the conversation is bothering you now. What had the other person said that seemed 'wrong' or whatever?

So, all of this is going on in your daily life, while you are 'awake,' so to speak. And when you sleep, you dream . . . which is a whole other state, but a state you go into naturally. When you sleep your conscious mind rests, as does your physical body. But your subconscious mind still plays while you sleep. Thoughts and ideas still percolate and float around, images

and thoughts merging, coming together and then parting again.

So, your awakened state is a natural
state, and your sleep state is a natural
state. So, wouldn't the hypnotic state
also be a natural state? Hmm. . .

The state of trance in hypnosis is no
more than your mind acutely focusing
on one thought or image as opposed
to another. You are simply in a more
relaxed frame of body and mind. Your
attention is more acute, more focused. Perhaps the colors in the vision
are more intense, etc. You might hear
the hypnotist's voice as just a voice in
the next aisle over in the grocery
store. You are only paying closer attention to this voice, while tuning out

or damping down all other sounds and images.

There is the REM (rapid eye movement) when you go into the trance state or hypnosis, similar to when you are on the edges of sleep (whether going into sleep or just before coming out of sleep).

And there is *day dreaming*. We've all had situations where we've been driving along on a beautiful spring day and had our thoughts wander to pleasant things, perhaps a past memory or thoughts of a future goal and what achieving that goal might feel like. Emotions and feelings are involved, along with thought. The particular memory you are thinking about might bring a flood of emotion.

You might be thinking of a loved one who has passed on and tears might begin to flow. Perhaps you might remember something funny that they had said and this thought brings a smile. And all the while you are driving.

So, isn't day dreaming similar to hypnosis, just without the hypnotist's voice directing you to focus on one particular thing over another? Are you not in a natural trance state? And how about reading? Have you ever been reading a book that the story was so absorbing that you were oblivious to someone knocking on the door? You were following along with the words that the author had written, and thoughts and images sprang forth in your mind. You were taking a mental journey, traveling along through what is the equivalent of a visualization that a hypnotist might describe. Some hypnotists actually use stories, or metaphors to present the suggestions that are most helpful to the subject. Often, the story might seem to be totally unrelated to anything, but the metaphor embedded within is picked up by the subject's subconscious mind. The mind makes the logical connection. The late, famed hypnotherapist, Dr. Milton Erickson has used the story of a meal to help a couple who were having sexual disfunction issues. Direct discussion of the issues was uncomfortable to the couple. So, Erickson used the story to get around this. It is really too much to go into here, but he used the differences of how each individual of the couple approached the meal. I believe he described the way the husband approached the food as being bold, attacking the food more energetically, whereas the woman approached the meal in a more timid and thoughtful way. He encouraged each to consider the other's approach and to appreciate the other's approach. He went on to describe the food and suggest the experience of enjoying the taste and act of eating the meal.

It all sounds a little odd, of course, but it worked. The subconscious mind of each made the logical connection. Probably due to the fact that each knew what they had come to the good doctor for, the reason behind the visit. And so, hypnosis is a natural phenomenon. So why does a person need to be moved or persuaded into the trance state?

Couldn't someone just read a visualization, story, or whatever? Aren't there parables in religious works? Doesn't the individual's mind pick up and absorb the proper message?

Here is an example of a visualization, one that can simply be read. Let your imagination play along.

So you are standing in a darkened room. There is a machine at the far end of the room that projects tennis balls at you. You don't have a tennis racket. You are to simply catch the balls and drop each one into a basket at your feet. Don't worry, these balls start out as actual tennis balls but turn into a more pliant foam before they get to you. Imagine Nerf balls (if they even make Nerf balls anymore). Foam balls. The balls are of varying colors: yellow, orange, and green. The room is very dark and you can only see the balls when they are within five feet of you, not before. To get you used to the idea and how to handle the balls flying at you, only one color will be used at first. After a few minutes, the next set will be a different color, and then the third. Your objective is to catch the balls and drop the green balls into one basket, then the yellow balls into another, and so on. Soon the balls are switching, flying at you. The speed picks up. Then you hear a voice over a loudspeaker telling you to only catch the orange balls, to let the others go. The balls coming at you are mixed. Then eventually, without warning, Rubik's cubes start coming at you, sporadically. These cubes are also made of a non-threatening foam substance by the time they reach you. All the same, you are supposed to catch the cubes and put them in a basket. You are directed as to which objects to catch. The voice coming over the speaker is guiding you. You follow along, crazy as the game is, with whatever the voice directs you to do. And now the instructions are to catch whichever item flashes at you when it gets close. All of the different colored balls interspersed with the random Rubik's cubes are coming at you at high speed. Now you are only concentrating on the items that emit a flash. The flash is only momentary so you have to pay close attention.

This all seems something like a game show of sorts, so let's add money to it. Whichever item flashes has money hidden inside. Are you more motivated now? How closely are you paying attention?

Now, suppose the items stop in mid air. The room is full of these balls and cubes, all of which are just hanging in mid air. There is an occasional flash, only for a second. You can see all of the items. You are to make your way over to the item that just flashed. You have to do this without bumping into any of the other items. To make things even more complex, the items that are suspended in air start randomly floating. If you bump into any of the other items while moving toward the item that flashed, the flashing item disappears. So, you are very careful now. And now, according to the voice, the items might contain positive messages. The cubes or balls that flash could hold money or a surge of feeling even. You might grab an item that had flashed and get an immediate surge of happiness, a distinct thrill of excitement might pass through you. You feel this feeling all throughout your body. This is a good, strong, happy and refreshing feeling. And then the lights come on and the items disappear and your friendly fellow hypnotist is coming toward you, smiling. Do you feel good?

Were you following along with the story as you read? Your mind probably didn't wander too much from the visualization, but why not? Well, because it was different. It was unique. At times it was confusing. It was a visualization that kept you wondering what in the world was going on, where was it all going? What was the point?

I'm quite sure you've gotten the point of it all. If you imagined yourself touching the items and feeling the surge of happiness or a simple thrill flowing through your body, well, you win. Good for you.

And all you did was read this visualization. I didn't relay or suggest any sort of relaxation or breathing exercises. There were no real instructions at all, nothing more than the suggestion that you allow your imagination to play along as you read along.

So, what do you think?

Is there such a thing as **hypnosis without hypnosis?**

Can you really just read a visualization and go into a light trance (is it even a trance at all?), absorbing whatever is presented and playing it all out in your imagination, accepting

all of the positive affirmations or suggestions therein?
I explore this idea in my book,
*Here There be Tygers! Hypnosis
through the Imagination.*

In Conclusion

I hope you have enjoyed reading this book. I also hope I have allayed any fears you might have regarding hypnosis. Also, I would like to believe you are much more informed on the subject after reading this book than you were before-hand. I would suggest that you keep learning about hypnosis by reading other books on the subject. There are thousands of books out there. I personally own between fifty and sixty books on hypnosis. Some are medical texts on the subject, others on research, some on the history of, etc. Most are very similar with only slight variations in technique or viewpoint.

Disclaimer/Warning

This book is for informational and entertainment purposes only. I offer it up for a way to suggestively and positively improve your life on a daily basis.

I hate to have to state the above, but there are those out there who will take something good and misuse it. I do not advise or condone such use or action.

Furthermore, I state again that if you suffer from epilepsy or any similar medical condition, or if you can't play video games without feeling dizzy or have a tendency to pass out, etc. DO NOT use any of the relaxation/visualization techniques or inductions offered up in this book. Do not try hypnosis at all if you suffer from any of these conditions.

Also, do not try to relieve any pain through suggestion without first consulting a medical doctor and having a thorough examination conducted to find out whether there might be an underlying cause.

It is best to consult with a medical doctor in any case before trying hypnosis. Check with the doctor to find out what his or her opinion might be regarding hypnosis, especially if you are in therapy for any mental condition or ailment. For example, if you are being treated for anxiety or depression, definitely consult your doctor.